Do Not Attempt This At Home

& Other Myths About Worship

Melody Lavin

Scripture taken from the NEW AMERICAN STANDARD BIBLE®, Copyright © 1960, 1962, 1963, 1968, 1971, 1972, 1973, 1975, 1977, 1995 by The Lockman Foundation. Used by permission. Noted as: NASB

Scripture quotations marked (ESV) are from the ESV® Bible (The Holy Bible, English Standard Version®), copyright © 2001 by Crossway, a publishing ministry of Good News Publishers. Used by permission. All rights reserved.

Scripture taken from the New King James Version®. Copyright © 1982 by Thomas Nelson. Used by permission. All rights reserved.

Do Not Attempt This At Home & Other Myths About Worship
ISBN: 978-1-939570-63-5

Copyright © 2016 Melody Lavin

Published by Word and Spirit Publishing.
P.O. Box 701403
Tulsa, Oklahoma 74170
wordandspiritpublishing.com

All rights reserved. This book or any portion thereof may not be reproduced or used in any manner whatsoever without the express written permission of the publisher except for the use of brief quotations in a book review.

Printed in the United States of America

TABLE OF CONTENTS

Introduction..v

Myth 1— Do not attempt this at home;
worshiping at church is enough.....................1

Myth 2— I'm not good enough to worship God..........9

Myth 3— I can't worship without the band,
and I don't have a good singing voice........15

Myth 4— It's all about me..21

Myth 5— Praise is just a fast song...............................25

Myth 6— It's God's job to draw me close....................33

Myth 7— If I can worship at home, then I can skip
the singing at church and come late............43

Myth 8— I need to tell myself to bless God; I need
to declare that I *will* worship Him..............47

What Now?..51

Introduction

I don't like long books. I don't seem to want to finish them. So I'll keep this short and to the point, and I'll give you something to think about.

If you're a believer, the best part of life can be when you spend time with God, honoring Him with your time and attention, enjoying His presence.

Worshiping God freely is one of the greatest gifts and privileges of the Christian life. No other religion can worship like ours—freely, in the One True God's presence. Every believer has the opportunity to worship.

Worship starts with knowing who God is and who you are. Without an understanding of who God is and who you are in Christ, worship becomes a formality—or worse, *just singing* at church.

This book is about true worship of God. It's not about the music; it's about what's in your heart. It's not about the form of worship; it's about your relationship with God.

Myth 1:

Do not attempt this at home; worshiping at church is enough

Reality:
Time with someone you love
shouldn't be limited to once a week

Think of a person—a living physical person, that you love to be with, your favorite person, the one who makes you laugh, who tells you the truth, and who loves you unconditionally. How often would you like to be with him or her?

What would you do to make time for that person in your schedule?

How do you talk to that person? Is a conversation always all about you or do you talk and listen?

Choose one:

    _____I'm always the talker

    _____The conversation is usually about me

    _____We both talk and we both listen

    _____I always just listen

Do you still want to have a friendship with your favorite person five years from now?

How will you keep that friendship going for the next five years?

Now, relate those thoughts and questions above to your relationship with God. Even if you don't know God well, what would your relationship/friendship look like in five years if you only talked with Him or listened to Him once

Myth 1

a week for an hour or two? It would be superficial. Sure, you would love Him, but would you really know Him?

You cannot truly—and will not want to—worship someone you do not know.[1] You won't want to worship an unknown god.

Is it possible to know God? Yes. To have a deep relationship with Him? Yes. How is that possible? He's God: busy, active, everywhere.

You can get to know God. He has revealed His character, His past actions, His form of speech, His thoughts and plans, and His interaction with those who serve and love Him. It's all in the Bible, which is God's words—God speaking, introducing Himself, telling you about Himself.

The more you come to know Him, the more you will want to worship Him. The more you worship Him, the deeper your relationship with Him will be.

It's like a loop: when you get to know God, you want to worship Him, and in worshiping Him, you come to know Him more, so you want to worship Him more.

Do Not Attempt This At Home & Other Myths About Worship

You come to know God in a personal way through worship—He reveals Himself as your focus is on Him.

There are levels of knowing someone. I know a woman named Cheryl because I've spent some time with her, but I know Andrea *better* because we've walked through the good and bad times together. I know her character. I trust her. But I know my husband, Mike, *best* because I spend every day with him. I know his likes and dislikes, his character, his personality, the sound of his voice, his history, his interaction with others. I know him well.

I know God—His likes and dislikes, His character, His personality, His heart, His will, the sound of His voice, the sense of His presence while being together as friends, the prompting of His Spirit, His interaction with others. I know Him very well. I've known Him my entire life.

How have I come to know God the Father? He introduced Himself to me through the Bible. Those are His words, His perspectives and thoughts. He communicates clearly. I've sensed His Holy Spirit as I've prayed and worshiped. I've felt His prompting, experienced His healing of my emotions, heard Him in my spirit convicting me of wrong

Myth 1

attitudes and sin, and I've known the sense of freedom that comes after repentance.

I know God because I've spent time with Him. I talk to Him throughout each day. I talk to God like I talk to all of my friends, with love and respect, listening for His response, wanting His perspective.

My close friends *deserve* to hear me tell them how wonderful they are. I see their value. I experience their care. I thank them repeatedly for what they've done. And I tell them how impressed I am with their skills, talents, and character. I tell them often because they are important to me, and they deserve to hear it. I value them. I love them.

If I can be authentic about my feelings toward my friends, I can be authentic toward God about my love and devotion for Him. Saying it aloud doesn't make me weak; it strengthens me because I'm telling God that He is: strong, faithful, reliable, capable, caring, thoughtful, always there for me, wise, and much more.

When I say His characteristics, I remember all the times that He acted on my behalf because of those characteristics. I remember when He was strong and wise, faithful and capable, thoughtful and comforting. That strengthens me; it makes me bold. When my worship is focused *on Him* and *about Him*, then He is blessed by what I say about Him. And I am strengthened through remembering that He doesn't change, and if He did something before, then He'll do it again.

The more I know *of Him*, the more in awe of Him I am. He's become my everything.

I've heard that you become like who you hang out with. Well, I want that. I want to be *like Him*.

The Apostle Paul wrote: "I count all things to be loss in view of the surpassing value of knowing Christ Jesus my Lord . . . . that I may know Him, and the power of His resurrection." Philippians 3:8,10 NASB

Paul wasn't writing about a simple acquaintance-type of relationship. He wanted to have a full, experience-based knowledge of God; the kind of relationship that is a result of walking through life together, experiencing everything together.

Myth 1

When you know God at that level, you see Him for who He really is, and you can't help but worship Him. Your worship will be of a depth that taps the core of who you are.

Ask yourself:

What have I allowed to keep me from developing my relationship with God?

What steps am I going to take so I can spend time with God?

Myth 2:

I'm not good enough to worship God

Reality:
You are a child of God,
empowered by His Spirit,
seated in Christ Jesus,
created for great things

Do you know who you are?

I am the wife of my husband, the mother of my children, the daughter of my parents. But that's not who I am.

Do Not Attempt This At Home & Other Myths About Worship

Someone greater defines me. I am a child of God, a covenant partner with God, a part of Christ's Body the Church, an ambassador for the Kingdom of Heaven, and a worshiper of God Almighty.

To truly know who we are we need to know what was provided for us when Jesus established the New Covenant, what we see in the New Testament.

There are things that are ours because of our covenant relationship with God; things that belong to us because we are *in Christ.* The Apostle Paul writes, "Therefore if anyone is in Christ, he is a new creature; the old things passed away; behold, new things have come." 2 Corinthians 5:17 NASB

Our relationship with God should not be summed up as a distant, future, life together in Heaven. We have a relationship with Him now.

Jesus told us to abide in Him (John 15:4-5). He told us to accept Him as Savior, to make Him Lord, to identify with His sacrifice, to receive His new life, to see ourselves as being in Him, to recognize that because of Him we can approach our Father God in worship and prayer with confidence, to accept His abundant life (John 10:10), and

Myth 2

to choose to abide in Him—take up active residence in Him and His life and to remain there.

The phrase, *abide in Me*, implies that there is no coming or going.

He said, "Abide in My love. If you keep My commandments, you will abide in My love . . . ." John 15:9-10 NASB

You are *in Christ Jesus*, and His Word is a part of you: it defines your morality and ethics, it provides the standards by which you live, and it strengthens and encourages and teaches you.

Choose to have a living, dynamic relationship with God the Father through Jesus Christ. This is a life where communication—both prayer and worship—is fluid, daily, easy, and authentic.

When you know who you are in Christ, then prayer becomes easy.

> Jesus said, "If you abide in Me, and My words abide in you, ask whatever you wish, and it will be done for you." John 15:7 NASB

Confidence is a product of knowing who you are in Christ Jesus.

11

Do Not Attempt This At Home & Other Myths About Worship

> "This is the confidence which we have before Him, that if we ask anything according to His will, He hears us. And if we know that He hears us in whatever we ask, we know that we have the requests which we have asked from Him." 1 John 5:14-15 NASB

When you know who you are in Christ, you can worship your Father God with confidence, knowing that through Jesus you are now a part of God's family. God's Spirit lives in you.

> "Do you not know that you are a temple of God and that the Spirit of God dwells in you?" 1 Corinthians 3:16 NASB

Focusing on speaking God's Word will keep us from begging and whining when we speak or sing to God. When we know what God says about us, we can pray prayers based on God's Word and worship Him with confidence.

Myth 2

——— Ask yourself: ———

Who am I in Christ? How do I know this?

When was the last time I read through the New Testament teachings of Paul, Peter, and James to understand what belongs to me through my covenant with God?

What New Covenant truths can I use as a filter for praise and worship songs that I sing to ensure that the songs agree with the New Covenant?

How effective is my Bible study time?

Myth 3:

I can't worship without the band, and I don't have a good singing voice

Reality:
Your words and your actions are enough

I sat on my bed one night, unable to sleep. I didn't have the answers I needed for some decisions. I had looked at everything logically, but I wasn't satisfied.

So in the darkness and quiet, when the noise of life was subdued, I worshiped. It was nighttime and I didn't sing. I spoke. I worshiped with my words, telling God that He was amazing, all-powerful, wonderful, more than marvelous, holy, worthy of all adoration. I told Him that I loved Him. I put my attention on Him, not on myself and what I needed. After some time, I was quiet.

In the quietness, He spoke. Then I knew what decisions I should make—what to do and what to say.

I worshiped alone, without a band or piano playing and someone telling me what to do or say. I spoke to God. Instead of asking for wisdom, I focused on Him and spoke about His greatness and compassion, expressing my love for Him.

Love is the basis of worship.

The most commonly used Greek word translated as *worship* and *worshiped* as an action in the New Testament is *proskuneo*, which can be defined as: *to kiss toward; showing unwavering devotion and adoration.* Our love for God is expressed to Him in a personal, heartfelt way through words and actions. We see this throughout the New Testament.

Myth 3

Worship begins in your spirit, at the center of who you truly are, and it is an *expression of your devotion to God.* You subject your body in reverence and adoration which can be shown through kneeling, bowing, falling prostrate—in short, *subjugating your body and showing submission* to a higher person/power—and your words of worship *focus on the person who is receiving the worship.*

Words of worship and demonstrations of worship are not limited to singing. In fact:

- Your spirit's attitude of worship comes first.
- Your physical actions reveal your spirit's attitude.
- Your worship that is expressed verbally is heard in the *words.*

Setting the words to music and singing them is an effective tool to glorify God since He created music, but **words of worship can be spoken**, they don't have to be sung.

Worship comes from your spirit and is expressed through your body, with your mind focused on God.

People who can't sing well and can't play an instrument can worship God. They can speak their love for God.

Do Not Attempt This At Home & Other Myths About Worship

Those who cannot speak can focus on God and, within themselves, tell Him how much they love Him. God sees the heart: "God sees not as man sees, for man looks at the outward appearance, but the LORD looks at the heart." 1 Samuel 16:7 NASB

> **Words of worship can be spoken, they don't have to be sung. You don't need the band.**

You may have been encouraged to think that you have to have guitars, a drummer, maybe a keyboardist, and some singers before you can worship. That's not true. If worship really is defined by what you say, the attitude of your spirit, and the submission and surrender of your body, then **you don't need the band**.

A band, an organ, a piano, or an ethnic instrument helps in corporate worship to keep musical time or direct the musical key of a song, or it can provide a background for contemplation. Instrumental music is a tool that inspires and can elevate the worship experience. But you can speak and sing words of worship without the band, on your own, wherever you are.

Ask yourself:

When will I make the time to give God my unwavering devotion?

What words will I say to Him?

Myth 4:

It's all about me

*Reality:
It's all about GOD*

Stop for a moment. Think about this: if worship is an expression of adoration and devotion to God, who should be the subject or focus of a worship song or words of worship?

If I'm worshiping God, my songs/words should be *about Him*. For example, "You are mighty. You are holy. You are faithful. You are worthy."

If I make God the focus of my attention, and sing/speak about who He is, I am truly worshiping.

Do Not Attempt This At Home & Other Myths About Worship

What about a song that says something like this? "I've fallen so many times. You pick me up. My heart is broken and I want your love. You pour out Your heart, and pull me past my pain. I rise again to worship You." Is that worship of God? Does it seem like the focus of the song is on the worshiper and not on the value and worth of the One who is being worshiped?

> Who should be the subject or focus of a worship song or words of worship?

Does it matter? Yes, it does. It's supposed to be worship *of God*, focused on Him, not worship of me and my failure or struggles.

Colossians 3:16 tells us that God's Word should dwell in us richly, and *out of that Word*, we should teach and admonish one another, and *out of that Word*, we should sing psalms and hymns, and spiritual songs (those are song styles), **singing with thankfulness** in our hearts **to God**.

Worship of God declares **who He is** and rejoices in it.

For example, in the song, *None Like You*, the focus is on Jesus, who He is.

Myth 4

(Verse 1) In all the world there is none like You, the only one who's faithful and true, worthy to be honored and adored, Jesus, You alone are Lord. You are the only blessed Son, whose Word is being spread abroad, and whose Kingdom will never cease, Jesus, You're the Prince of Peace.

(Chorus) And Your Name will be exalted, the Word of God who is victorious. Lord of Lords, You rule in power. You are glorious. Seated high above the heavens with Your Father in all glory. You will reign with Him forever for your Kingdom has no end. It has no end.

(Verse 2) You were God in the form of man. You were the sacrificial Lamb, whose blood has set mankind free. Jesus, You are Liberty. The only True and Living God, who was sent to make God's Kingdom come, and on earth His will to be done. Jesus, You're the Holy One.

None Like You © 2000 Melody Lavin,
ASCAP, CCLI song # 4028963

Let's commit ourselves to worshiping God, putting our attention and our words (and song words) on Him. Sing and speak to Him about His attributes and character, and express your love for Him.

It's not about you; it's about Him.

Ask yourself:

In what ways have I been self-focused in worship?

How will I change the songs I sing and the words I speak to God so *He* is the focus of my worship?

Myth 5:

Praise is just a fast song

Reality:
Praise of God is declaring what God has done and thanking Him for it

Praise of God is a response to what He has done on the earth, and for us and within us. "Let us continually offer up a sacrifice of praise to God, that is, the fruit of lips that give thanks to His name." Hebrews 13:15 NASB

Have you ever wondered what to say to praise God? The Bible is full of words that praise God, words that tell what

He has done. When we choose to rejoice and to praise God, these are the words that should be in our mouths.

The prophet Isaiah wrote of God's declarations about Himself:

> "I, even I, am the LORD; and there is no savior besides Me. It is I who have declared and saved and proclaimed, and there was no strange god among you; so you are My witnesses, declares the LORD, and I am God. Even from eternity I am He; and there is none who can deliver out of My hand, I act and who can reverse it?" Isaiah 43:11-13 NASB

> "I, the LORD, am the maker of all things, stretching out the heavens by Myself, and spreading out the earth all alone." Isaiah 44:24 NASB

> "There is no one besides Me. I am the LORD, and there is no other, the One forming light and creating darkness." Isaiah 45:6-7 NASB

> "I, the LORD, speak righteousness declaring things that are upright." Isaiah 45:19 NASB

Myth 5

"For as the rain and the snow come down from heaven, and do not return there without watering the earth and making it bear and sprout, and furnishing seed to the sower and bread to the eater; so will My word be which goes forth from My mouth; it will not return to Me empty, without accomplishing what I desire, and without succeeding in the matter for which I sent it."
Isaiah 55:10-11 NASB

I want to encourage you to open your mouth and move your tongue. Speak the words from those Scriptures as praise to God like this: "God, I praise You. You have created the stars and placed them in the heavens. You've been just and faithful in everything that You do. You have all power, and You show it in Your creation and in Your faithfulness to fulfill Your Word to us. You have saved us and made us Your own. There is no one else like You. You are above all else, and what You do is powerful!"

When we see the big picture of who God is, what He's done, and what the Bible says about Him, we'll recognize that He's worthy of praise. The Bible tells us about God's acts of strength, about His unfailing love for us, about His faithfulness to His covenant with us.

Praise of God is a response to what He's done within us. Through the power of His Spirit, He created us to look like Him. "Therefore if anyone is in Christ, he is a new creature; the old things passed away; behold, new things have come." 2 Corinthians 5:17 NASB And the Father God placed His Spirit within us at the new birth, at salvation. "Do you not know that you are a temple of God and that the Spirit of God dwells in you?" 1 Corinthians 3:16 NASB

That's cause for joy, for praise.

You could say, "God, I praise You for the work You've done in my life. You made me new inside. No one else could have done that. You gave me Your Spirit. You deserve praise. Thank You for Your kindness and Your love for me."

When Jesus healed a blind man, the people saw the miracle and began to praise God for what was done. God received the credit for what had happened.

> "And Jesus said to him, 'Receive your sight; your faith has made you well.' Immediately he regained

Myth 5

his sight and began following Him, glorifying God; and when all the people saw it, they gave praise to God." Luke 18:42-43 NASB

Praising God should be as natural as breathing. Just say "Thanks!" to God. Open your mouth and boast about Him and what He's done. Give Him the credit. "I will bless the LORD at all times; His praise shall continually be in my mouth. My soul shall make its boast in the LORD; the humble shall hear of it and be glad." Psalm 34:1-2 NKJV

I am a fairly typical parent. I like to tell people what my children have accomplished. I think that my children are special and wonderful, and I want my friends and family to know that. So, I tell them about my children.

God is even more special and wonderful. You and I should boast about Him. We should tell everyone about all of the exciting things that God has done, what He's accomplished, and how wonderful He is. We should tell them that God is trustworthy, and then tell them why He's trustworthy—tell them what He's done.

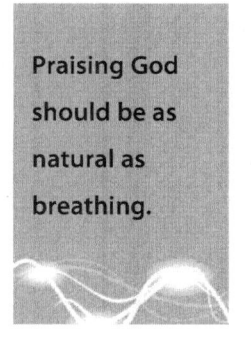

> Praising God should be as natural as breathing.

God said, "the people whom I formed for Myself will declare My praise." Isaiah 43:21 NASB

So I say, "With my mouth I will give thanks abundantly to the LORD; and in the midst of many I will praise Him." Psalm 109:30 NASB

Here is an example of a song that praises God in its verses; the focus is on boasting about what God has done. The chorus is worship that exalts who God is. The song is titled *Source of Life*.

(Verse 1) Before the world was made, You were there in infinite glory, with all radiant light, in all splendor. You spoke and life began, worlds became, creation's story unfurled, and heavens declared the wonder, for

(Chorus) You are the source of life, creator of Heaven and Earth. You are the most awesome God. You're glorious.

(Verse 2) Father of lights sent the Light to the world, clothed in flesh to dispel sin's darkness. Your plan and pleasure revealed in Your gift. The

Myth 5

promise fulfilled by the love You have shown in great kindness, for

(Chorus) You are the source of life, creator of Heaven and Earth. You are the most awesome God. You're glorious.

Source of Life © 2000 Melody Lavin,
ASCAP, CCLI song # 4029027

——— Ask yourself: ———

In what ways have I truly been praising God?

When was the last time I thanked God for the things He has done in my life?

How can I change to become *continually* thankful?

Myth 6:

It's God's job to draw me close

Reality:
You do it

At times following a church service I've heard people say, "Great service! God was really present." We sensed His presence and glory, experienced it and participated in what He wanted to do in that moment, and then we left the awareness of His presence to focus solely on our natural lives.

We've settled for a brief experience and missed the reality that it can always be like that; we can stay in the presence of God.

Do Not Attempt This At Home & Other Myths About Worship

It's time to stay at God's throne, in His presence in intimate fellowship and communion on a daily basis, instead of entering and leaving His presence Sunday mornings and periodically when we have a need.

Hebrews 4:16 says, "Therefore let us draw near with confidence to the throne of grace, that we may receive mercy and find grace to help in time of need." NASB But the Scripture does not say that to reach the throne of grace requires a long journey, or that it takes a long time to get there. It's a matter of causing your body to participate with what your spirit wants to do and focusing your mind on God.

> It's time to stay in God's presence continually on a daily basis. It's time to be who we really are.

You come close or draw near to God boldly, not timidly, not with fear but with joy and reverence and confidence because of Jesus (see Hebrews 7:19, 25; 10:19-22).

We also need to remember what Paul wrote in Ephesians 1:20 and 2:6: Jesus is seated at the right hand of the Father God, and we are seated *with Him* and *in Him*. Your spirit (the real you) is *in Christ,* and

Myth 6

He is *in you*. Your position in the Church, the Body of Christ, is *in Christ* (see 2 Corinthians 5:17; 1 Corinthians 1:30; Galatians 3:26-28; Ephesians 2:6). You are *in Him* and He is seated at the right hand of the Father (see Hebrews 8:1). So, you are seated *in Christ* at the right hand of the Father.

Now **live your life in that reality**. Make your body respond to that reality. Cause your mind to think according to that reality.

Drawing near to or fellowshipping closely with God can be *instantaneous*. James 4:8 encourages you to draw near to or fellowship with God and He will fellowship with you. Decide and do it.

When my oldest son first started school, I would wait for him outside the school building after school so I could walk home with him. He would run out of the building straight for me. My arms were wide open, and he would throw himself at me and say "Hi, Mom!"

That's the way I approach my relationship with God. His arms are always wide open. I throw myself into His arms and say, "Hi, Father!" I am completely abandoned and authentic with Him—all the time.

Some of the songs people sing and some prayers that I've heard prayed beg God to do the action: to draw us close to Himself. He says to us: You need to respond to what I've done for you, respond in faith by drawing near to Me, take that step toward Me in faith and begin to worship.

The New Testament is full of directives for the believer that require action. For example:

Colossians 3:1-2: You are to seek the things that are above. You are to set your mind, your focus, on things that are above, not on things that are on earth.

Matthew 6:33: You are to seek God first, before all else.

Colossians 3:12-15: You are to put on compassionate hearts, kindness, humility, meekness, patience, forgiveness, and love. You are to allow Christ's peace to rule in your heart.

1 Peter 3:11: You are to seek peace and pursue it.

Romans 14:19: You are to pursue what creates peace, unity and encourages (builds up) others.

Myth 6

Philippians 2:3-4: You are to value unity and work to accomplish it. You are to care for others.

Philippians 4:4-6: You are to rejoice and to pray with thanks to God.

Philippians 4:8: You are to think about what is pure and lovely and commendable.

Hebrews: 12:1-2: You are to look to Jesus, keep your focus on Him, and live your life knowing that God is your strength.

It seems to me that you and I are the ones who are to be active, to initiate, to change, to pursue and seek, to determine, to follow. We act. We don't beg; we act. We speak. We listen. We obey. We reap the results of freedom and blessing in our lives.

So why do we, as a Church, think that it's appropriate to speak a prayer or sing a song that begs our Father God to draw us to Himself when He expects us to act and move toward Him? He acted first, sending His Son and establishing a relationship with us through Jesus. We act on the basis of that relationship and come close to Him.

My children never hesitate to find me and spend time with me. Regardless of where I am, they will find me. When they were young, they wouldn't give up until we were snuggled into a chair reading a book, laughing together on the piano bench, tickling each other on the grass, or talking quietly about important things in the quietness of a room. My children want to be with me, and I want to be with, talk to, and laugh with them. We seek each other, and we take time for each other. It's our lifestyle.

Even now that my children are older, they don't beg me to hug them. They know that my arms are always open and ready for hugging. My children move toward me, even just one step, and their arms are open and so are mine. Before you know it, we're embracing closely. We're family.

Come to God to fellowship. Seek Him. Speak and sing from your heart, release what's inside. Go beyond your physical body and its desires. Ignore your physical hunger or discomfort and run to *Him!*

You may not want to leave your comfort zone. You may like to remain aloof or untouched. There's a risk in fellowship with God; He may want you to change an area of your life. People often resist change, but God knows you

Myth 6

personally. He knows your potential. He wants to help you reach your potential just as a loving parent sacrifices and works to enable a child to reach his or her potential in life.

We don't need to fear what God will say to us when we fellowship with Him. Most often He will say the words we all want to hear: "I love you."

Have you ever seen someone cry when God speaks to them through a minister, and He says, "I love you My child"? It's as if the person is amazed that God hears, knows, and loves them.

A child of God who is amazed at God's words of love through a minister is a child of God who spends no time with God.

When I would tuck my youngest son into bed at night, he would throw his arms around me, squeeze my neck, and say, "I love you Mom more than I can say. It's so big in me." Those words meant more to me than any promise to do good or any gift. This same little guy would jump off the school bus and run headlong into my arms. I was covered by squeezes and kisses. I have been loved unconditionally, boundlessly, exuberantly.

Have I, God's child, loved Him in the same way? Have I raced toward Him and lifted my hands toward Him and shouted, "I love you"? Have I murmured to Him at night, "I love you Father more than I can say. It's so big in me"? That's family fellowship. That's the heart of a child. Love expressed and received between you and God is the foundation of your fellowship with Him.

> Love expressed and received between you and God is the foundation of your fellowship with Him.

You are God's child. You are a spirit being created in the image of God, who is a Spirit. This love expressed—this fellowship, this worship and focus on God—pleases Him without end. God wants His children to worship Him in Spirit and in truth. Jesus said, "But an hour is coming, and now is, when the true worshipers will worship the Father in spirit and truth; for such people **the Father seeks to be His worshipers**. God is spirit, and those who worship Him must worship in spirit and truth." John 4:23, 24 NASB (Boldface added)

God is seeking *true* worshipers. God is looking for people who will enter and stay in His presence and rejoice in

Myth 6

Him—people who are genuine in their worship. God does not want just an outward expression; He wants your true nature to be expressed. He wants worship from your heart that involves your body and soul. Empty words and conforming actions don't please Him. He delights in love expressed exuberantly and wholeheartedly.

---- **Ask yourself:** ----

How have I determined to go beyond a continual focus on my feelings, my body's desires and the situations that I face each day?

In what ways have I determined to keep my focus on God throughout the day?

What can I change in my life so I remain in God's presence by living a Holy Spirit-led, Spirit-directed life?

Myth 7:

If I can worship at home, then I can skip the singing at church and come late

Reality:
When your personal worship life is meaningful, corporate worship in church is much more than just singing together

Are you that guy that stands like a stiff tree at church, totally disengaged? Or are you uncomfortable with showing any response in church so you come late and sit in the back and hope that no one notices you?

Frankly, you get out of a church service what you put into it. Your expectation level determines whether you'll be satisfied with the experience.

Think of your favorite sports team and what the coach would say before a game or match. He would encourage the team to take the skills perfected in practice to the field and give 100% attention to the game. Focus on the opportunity to give your all. Don't hold back anything. Be completely immersed.

And yet we come to a church service and expect the worship team or director to make us want to worship. It's almost as if we dare that leader to influence our emotions and impress us with their presentation so we're inspired enough to worship.

That's wrong. Where in the Scriptures does it tell you to come together as a part of Christ's Body and to passively stand or sit there until someone cajoles you enough that

Myth 7

you reluctantly begin to sing or focus your attention on God?

In corporate worship, the worship team's job is not to entertain you but to provide an environment in which you can *continue* your worship of God and worship with others.

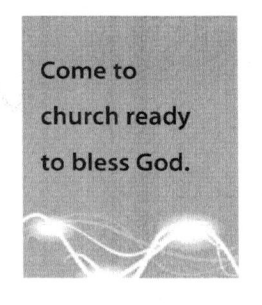

Come to church ready to bless God.

We need to change. We need to *come to church ready.* If we have a personal worship relationship with God on a daily basis, then our time together in corporate worship in a church service or gathering should be the *overflow of our personal worship.*

That means that we have to care enough to begin preparing ourselves spiritually before a church service, singing and/or speaking our praise and worship of God, getting out of bed and getting ready on time, and choosing to avoid becoming angry at our spouses or children or the drivers of other cars.

We need to understand that when we are worshiping our God together, we are being what God created us to be: the Body of Christ, the Church, exemplifying true unity in the Spirit.

Meaningful corporate worship begins at home, in our personal worship of God, and it's magnified when we worship together.

Ask yourself:

What do I need to change so I will arrive at church ready to participate?

What have I wanted from my time together with other believers?

Myth 8:

I need to tell myself to bless God; I need to declare that I will worship Him

Reality:
Just do it

Do you pull out your checkbook or open your internet browser to make a mortgage payment and boldly declare, "I will make a mortgage payment! Oh my soul and body, make a mortgage payment!" No. You just do it. You write and mail the check or you make the payment online.

You don't announce it; you just do it.

When you know who you are in Christ, and you live life in constant communion with your Father God, you won't have to say or sing to yourself: "Bless the Lord oh my soul" or "I will worship." You will just do it.

You won't need a warm-up; you'll open your mouth and say or sing, "I bless You Father for You are mighty, faithful, strong, holy, and awesome." You won't say or sing "I *will* worship"; you'll open your mouth and worship!

> Take a moment and say this: "God, You are marvelous. You have done great things. You rescue sinners and abundantly bless Your children. You are my Redeemer, Healer, Baptizer, Deliverer, Savior, Comforter. You have healed the lame and the blind and raised the dead. You rescue the destitute and give strength to the weary. I honor You. I adore You. I worship You. You are holy and full of justice and Truth. You are Light and Life, the Creator and my Father."

Myth 8

Jump in and worship and praise God. Open your mouth and begin to bless God.

——— Ask yourself: ———

What words have I said lately to bless God?

What words will I say to bless Him from this point onward?

What Now?

You can have an amazing relationship with God—one where you sense His presence daily and remain connected with Him. It's dependent on whether you are willing to be authentic with Him, transparent and open, holding nothing back.

Worshiping and praising God isn't difficult; it's easy communication with God that enriches your life and reminds you of who He is since your focus is on Him.

Get to know Him by reading your Bible. Then honor Him by saying thanks for all He's done and all you anticipate He will do. Keep your attention on Him. You'll be surprised at how quickly the depth of your relationship with Him will change.

Don't wait. Start now.

NOTES

Myth 1

1. Melody Lavin, *Effective Worship-Leading Workshop.* (1999, 2015), 6.

Melody Lavin is an international teacher and worship clinician. Melody and her husband, Michael, direct Victorious Living Ministries International, Incorporated™, combining practical Bible training with compassionate outreach.

Melody has established and directed Bible Schools internationally, worked with pastors to establish Bible training programs in their churches, authored Bible School curriculum, served as a worship pastor, and trained ministers internationally. Melody is a graduate of Rhema Bible Training College with a concentration in music ministry. She has degrees in Theology and Biblical Studies from Vision Christian Bible College & Seminary.

Melody has extensive experience working with contemporary worship teams, strengthening their skills, and focusing their ministry.

Worship training with Melody is available for your church or music group.

> ***Effective Worship-Leading Workshop*** — An 8-hour workshop that covers foundational, scriptural and practical/musical topics for effective worship-leading.

Worship Clinic — Fully customized, practical training that increases a worship team's musical and worship-leading skills.

A Worship Challenge — A seminar specifically designed for senior and associate pastors, worship ministers, worship team members, choir directors, choir members, and musicians who serve in leading people in worship.

Melody also is available to minister in your church or to your group with seminars and practical workshops, in church services, and for retreats.

Melody's experience, diverse background, and humor provide a fresh perspective of life and ministry.

Email: melody@vlmi.org
Website: www.vlmi.org
Blog: worship.expert